To my wife, who always believes in me.

To my children and grandchildren, who are
a gift from God.

To the Glory of Jesus Christ who, by His
grace, has made me what I am.

Genesis 1

Creation & Christmas – Dec 22, 2010

Genesis 1:1 NIV84

> "In the beginning God created the heavens and the earth."

This is perhaps the single most important verse in the Bible. Without it the concept of sin is meaningless, the story of the Fall of man in Eden becomes the story of a cosmic bully, and the idea of redemption and grace are empty ideas at best. If, however, God created everything that exists then sin has to do with destroying a special creation. If God is creator, then the fall becomes about defacing God's unique work of art. If God is creator, then grace and redemption have to do with a benevolent creator taking the initiative to restore relationship. This very first verse of the Bible is foundational to everything that follows. With it the cross has meaning and Christmas becomes even more significant. Without it they're just empty religion.

Creator, Father, what an amazing thought that I can call you, the almighty creator my Father. May I not lose the wonder of that truth in the busyness and glitter of the season.

By His grace,
Rick Weinert

Genesis 2

Marriage – Dec 24, 2010

Genesis 2:23 NIV84

> "This is now bone of my bones and flesh of my flesh; she shall be called 'woman,' for she was taken out of man."

You can't read this passage and take away the idea that man is superior to woman unless you bring that lens to the text. The next verses indicate that the idea here is oneness and unity, not superiority and control.

Our culture has put us in competition with each other when God's intent was that we compliment one another as husband and wife. Because of the Fall, complimenting one another can sometimes be complicated, but that's no excuse for competition or control. By God's grace a marriage can be what God intended.

Father, may our marriage, the marriages of our children, and ultimately those of our grandchildren honor you by reflecting your original intent. May we truly understand what it means to be one.

By His grace,
Rick Weinert

Genesis 3

Christmas & Genesis 3 – Dec 25, 2010

In Genesis 3, there are so many parallels with the Christmas story. Verse 15 is why the savior came, "And I will put enmity between you and the woman, and between your offspring and hers; he will crush your head, and you will strike his heel." Jesus, the seed of the woman, came to crush the Serpent's head.

Verse 16 is what Mary was experiencing in the stable that night when Jesus was born, "To the woman he said, "I will greatly increase your pains in childbearing; with pain you will give birth to children.""

Verse 21 is what Jesus offered us through his death, "The Lord God made garments of skin for Adam and his wife and clothed them." By grace, through faith, we are clothed with the life of the one who died for us.

In verse 22 man is kept away from the Tree of Life. "And the Lord God said, "The man has now become like one of us, knowing good and evil. He must not be allowed to reach out his hand and take also from the tree of life and eat, and live forever."" But because Jesus came, we believers will eat of the Tree of Life in the New Heavens and New Earth.

In verse 23 man was banned from the Garden, but because Jesus came believers will be welcomed into the City at the center of the New Heavens and New Earth. The New Earth itself is a whole new garden. "So the Lord God banished him from the Garden of Eden to work the ground from which he had been taken."

In verse 24 an angel guarded the way to the Tree of Life, But when Jesus who is life was born, his birth was announced by a host of angels. "After he drove the man out, he placed on the east side of the Garden of Eden cherubim and a flaming sword flashing back and forth to guard the way to the tree of life."

What an incredible story! Father, thank you that the story didn't end in Genesis 3, but never let me forget that it begins there. Because of Jesus ours is a merry Christmas.

By His grace,
Rick Weinert

Genesis 4

Sin – Dec 26, 2010

As I read the story of the first murder, in Genesis 3, I'm struck by how normal Cain's life is. He has a wife and children. His descendents do normal things like raising livestock, making music, and working with metals. Yet two things stand out in stark contrast. First, because of Cain's violence against his brother, he loses the lifestyle he cared most about. He could no longer be a gardener. Second is the exponential growth of sin. Cain killed his brother and tried to hide it. His descendent, Lamech, kills someone and brags about it. Sin always has its consequences, and it always grows like dandelions.

Father, thank you for your grace and forgiveness. Forgive me for those times I have thought a little compromise was harmless. May I live in holiness and peace, and may we see a heritage of faith and holiness follow us.

By His grace,
Rick Weinert

Genesis 5
Hope – Dec 27, 2010

There are two thoughts that stand out to me as I read Genesis 5. First is the idea of "likeness". Man was created in the likeness of God according to verse 1. In verse 3 Adam had a son in his own likeness. I'm not sure if that is to indicate that something has changed, the Fall perhaps, or if it is to indicate that the likeness of God hasn't disappeared. Although I've heard the first idea taught I'm almost inclined to go with the latter idea. It fits with the second thought that struck me in this chapter.

The second thought is found in verse 29. "He named him Noah and said, "He will comfort us in the labor and painful toil of our hands caused by the ground the Lord has cursed."" Here again I'm not sure how I should take this. Is this a prophecy about the ark, or is it irony that the one who alone, with his immediate family, will survive the flood, while everyone else will lose their lives, is said to bring comfort?

Both of these thoughts seem to have two possible meanings and I'm not sure which way to take either of them. I'm inclined to believe that these are statements of hope following the threefold negative story that precedes this chapter. In chapter 3 we have the record of the Fall of man. In chapter 4 we have the story of the first murder. At the end of chapter 4 we find Lamech bragging about the second murder recorded. It's time for some good news, and we find it in chapter 5. The image of God has not disappeared. Adam was created in the image of God and passed on that image to his son Seth. In the pain following the fall there is the promise of comfort in the person of Noah.

If this is an accurate understanding, then both of these men becomes pictures of, or hints toward, Christ. In Christ we become "partakers of the divine nature"; the image of God is restored (2 Peter 1: 4). Christ is our comfort and rest. "My yoke is easy and my burden is light" he told us. "There remains a rest for the people of God" Hebrews 4 instructs us. Jesus is that rest.

In chapter 5 of Genesis, then, I find hope. Father thank you that you have never abandoned us, but always offer hope. I rest in that truth.

By His grace,
Rick Weinert

Genesis 6

Righteous & Blameless – Dec 28, 2010

Genesis 6:8 NIV84

"But Noah found favour in the eyes of the Lord."

> "But I will establish my covenant with you, and you will enter the ark — you and your sons and your wife and your sons' wives with you."

Noah found favour in Gods eyes. Not Noah and his sons and their wives, just Noah. Yet Noah, his wife, their sons, and their wives are all saved from the flood. The influence of a godly individual in a family, a community, or perhaps even a nation can be greater than we realize. Noah's family was saved because of Noah. It makes me wonder how often a family, community, or country has been blessed, or saved from judgement because of the presence of godly individuals.

Noah is described, in verse 9, as being both righteous and blameless. "Righteous" refers to his relationship with God. "Blameless" refers to his relationship to people. It makes me wonder how influential my own life is. Father, may I be the kind of person whose very presence might divert your judgment from those around me. May I be the presence of Christ wherever I am.

By His grace,
Rick Weinert

Genesis 7

Holiness & Destruction – Dec 29, 2010

Genesis 7:23 NIV84

> "Every living thing on the face of the earth was wiped out; men and animals and the creatures that move along the ground and the birds of the air were

wiped from the earth. Only Noah was left, and those with him in the ark."

This is the consequence of doing things our way. This destruction is where sin leads us. Most "end of the world" movies have high ground somewhere, or someone discovers the secret solution and saves the world at the last minute. We have a hard time accepting complete annihilation, yet there is coming a day when this world will come to an end. Next time it won't be a flood, and it won't just be those creatures with the breath of life that will be destroyed. The heavens and earth will melt. Even then, the good news is that's not the end, for there will be a new heavens and a new earth, a new Genesis.

When you think of the destruction, though, you have to ask, "Why?" The answer, of course, is that if we truly understood the nature of God and the horror of our sin we wouldn't be asking. Perhaps Genesis 6:6 helps us understand just a bit, "The Lord was grieved that he had made man on the earth, and his heart was filled with pain." The benevolent creator's heart was filled with pain as he watched what mankind had done to his earth and to each other, his special creations.

Father, I have a feeling that I haven't taken sin nearly seriously enough in my own life. Forgive me. May the words of my mouth and the meditations of my heart be acceptable in your sight Lord. May I reflect your holiness in all I do.

By His grace,
Rick Weinert

Genesis 8

Never Forgotten – Dec 31, 2010

Genesis 8:1 NIV84

"But God remembered Noah and all the wild animals and the livestock that were with him in the ark, and he sent a wind over the earth, and the waters receded."

God never forgets us. In the midst of the most difficult circumstances God hasn't forgotten, nor abandoned us. He not only remembered Noah, but also all the animals. As the song goes, "His eye is on the sparrow, and I know he watches me." Not only did God remember Noah and the animals, but the chapter ends with the promise that never again will he destroy all living creatures.

Father, in my darkest, loneliest times you are there. Thank you for that assurance. I rest in your promise that you will never forsake me. In you I find peace no matter what storms howl around me.

By His grace,
Rick Weinert

Genesis 9

Mission & Division – Jan 3, 2011

Genesis 9 starts with God blessing Noah, and twice instructing him to "be fruitful and increase in number; multiply on the earth and increase upon it." The chapter ends with Noah cursing one of his sons. That's not multiplication. Sin is still very much alive.

As I write this, it suddenly strikes me how much this sounds like the church. We've been commissioned to be fruitful, multiply, and fill the earth. We were told to make disciples throughout the whole earth, yet much of our mission gets waylaid by sin and divisiveness. We spend more time cursing each other than multiplying.

Was the curse justified by Ham's sin. Yes, but unfortunately the result was a distraction from their mission to be fruitful.

Was Ham's action the first move away from mission? No. Noah's drunkenness did little to fill the earth. It's easy to blame those with the most obvious sins, those teaching wrong doctrine, those excusing sin, those being divisive, but more often the truth is that we lost sight of our mission long before these things became an issue. In some cases it may even be that these things became issues because we lost sight of our mission.

Father, I have to confess that mission is not always on the top of my priority list. My own comfort, or some other equally noxious motivation often obscures the real purpose for which you left us here. May I get back on task today.

By His grace,
Rick Weinert

Genesis 10-11

A Memorial – Jan 5, 2011

I just read Genesis 10-11 several times. They contain the genealogies of Noah's children, and the story of the Tower of Babel. What caught my eye was the motivation for building the tower.

Genesis 11:4 NIV84

> "Then they said, "Come, let us build ourselves a city, with a tower that reaches to the heavens, so that we may make a name for ourselves and not be scattered over the face of the whole earth.""

The "not be scattered" part I get. What caught my attention was the "make a name for ourselves" piece. We were created in the image of God, and there is always that drive for significance within us. When I first moved to a city, I was struck by the fact that I was surrounded by buildings and concrete that all pointed to their designers and builders. There were magnificent buildings, unique and creative art pieces, and massive structures all of which spoke volumes about both the skill and creativity of those involved in their construction. Our world contains huge sculptures, structures and memorials that leave us wondering about their creators, things like the Easter Island carvings, the pyramids, Incan and Mayan structures, Stonehenge, etc. There is a sense in which these all served to make a name for their creators.

We still wrestle with the question, "What will we leave behind us?" Will we leave memorial stones in a cemetery? Will we leave buildings or businesses? Will we leave a heritage of faith and holiness? Father, if I am remembered may it not be for dead buildings and monuments, but for living faith and genuine holiness. May my life leave in its wake people who have been influenced for your glory by my life.

By His grace,
Rick Weinert

Genesis 12

Faith – Jan 6, 2011

Genesis 12:3a NIV84

> "I will bless those who bless you, and whoever curses you I will curse"

God promised to bless and protect Abram, yet when he made the trek to Egypt he felt it necessary to tell a lie about his wife. He claimed she was his sister in order to protect himself. Three questions come to mind as I read this. First, I wonder why his first priority wasn't to protect his wife instead of himself. It's possible that he felt he was between a rock and a hard place. That is, if he stayed in Canaan he felt that he, his wife, and all of those under his authority would starve, yet he knew it was potentially dangerous to go to Egypt. Further, he may have felt that Sarai would be okay in

Egypt no matter what happened. If they knew she was his wife they might kill him and take all that was his, but she would be the wife of a king. If they thought she was his sister they would form an alliance with him and she would still end up being the wife of the king. Then there was the off chance that nothing would happen. All of that to say that maybe he felt like he had no other choice. That being said, it was no excuse and yet God protected him.

The second question that comes to mind is, "Didn't he trust God to do what He had promised?" God had said that he would bless Abram, bless those that bless him, and curse those that curse him. So, why did he feel that he needed to go to Egypt, and why did he feel the need to lie? We all have those times when the threats that face us seem much more real than the God who promised to care for us. Perhaps that's what happened with Abram. He is still in the process of getting to know this God who covenanted with him. What he is beginning to learn is that God will do what he said he would do. We often learn best the faithfulness of God in our darkest hours.

The final question builds on the last. Did Abram feel like he needed to help God keep his word. How often we say, "I believe God will take care of me," but then we spend our hours worrying and fretting, or scheming about how to bring about that which God said he would do. This is not a call to inactivity, but clearly we can't help God save us. Do we really think we can help him do anything else in our lives? Willing, submissive obedience is one thing. Feeling like we need to help God with a little push is another. That's like calling a tow truck and then pushing for all we're worth once the tow truck is hooked up to our car. Are we really accomplishing anything except wearing ourselves out?

Father, I've felt like Abram more times than I care to admit. I've made poor choices because I felt like I had no other choice. I've claimed to trust you only to feel that the circumstances I was facing were more real to me than you were. I've acted as though you could only fulfill your word and your promises if you had a little extra push from me. Father, I'm learning, but I have a long way to go. Thank you that you continue to faithfully guide and guard in spite of me, just as you did Abram and Sarai. Ultimately, I rest in that truth.

By His grace,
Rick Weinert

Genesis 13

Character – Jan 7, 2011

In Genesis 13 we get a glimpse of Abram's and Lot's character. Abram is a peacemaker. When conflict breaks out between his servants and Lot's, he offers a solution. He gives Lot first choice as to which part of the land to claim. Lot's character becomes clear as he chooses the choice land for his flocks.

We see a hint as to their futures when the sinfulness and eventual destruction of Sodom is mentioned. These are the people Lot chose to live among. Abram, on the other hand, is promised, by God, that he will eventually possess all the land.

Their future is determined partly by the fact that God has already entered into covenant with Abram, but also by the character revealed in their choices. Father, may the choices I make, the motives of my heart, and the words and actions I produce reflect the character of Christ.

By His grace,
Rick Weinert

Genesis 14

Stuff – Jan 11, 2011

Genesis 14:21 NIV84

> The king of Sodom said to Abram, "Give me the people and keep the goods for yourself."

Abram had just delivered his nephew Lot, Sodom, and Sodom's allies from King Kedorlaomer. In gratitude the king of Sodom offered Abram the spoils of war. Abram's response was interesting. After tithing the spoils to Melchizedek, he refused to keep anything for himself. I fear that I would have been inclined to keep the spoils and neglect the tithe.

Father, we get so wrapped up in our "stuff" that we lose sight of you. Forgive us for this. May we always remember that what we have is from you, and who we are is from you. May we honor you in all we do. May we never live as slaves to our possessions.

By His grace,
Rick Weinert

Genesis 15

Unfailing Faithfulness – Jan 12, 2011

In Genesis 15, Abram is struggling to believe God's promises. In response, God reiterates his promises and enters into a covenant with Abram to reassure him. As a part of that covenant he says, in verse 13, "Know for certain that your descendants will be strangers in a country not their own, and they will be enslaved and mistreated four hundred years."

Now what kind of reassurance is that? God is saying that even when things look out of control, the next generations can be assured that God is in control. He has not forgotten his promises. He has his purposes, and he will keep his word. They could rest assured that God had not forgotten His promises.

Father, when things feel out of control it is sometimes difficult to remember that you are still there. Thank you for this reminder. I rest in your unfailing faithfulness.

By His grace,
Rick Weinert

Genesis 16

Waiting on God – Jan 13, 2011

The story of Sarai, Abram and Hagar, in Genesis 16, is fascinating. Sarai hatches a plan to help God fulfill his promise. Abram goes along with the plan. When the plan succeeds all relationships break down. Pregnant Hagar despises her mistress. Sarai blames Abram. Abram approves of Hagar's mistreatment. And the final result? Broken relationships, a scenario of conflict for the future between Ishmael, Hagar and Abram's son, and others, and Abram and Sarai are still waiting for God to keep his promise.

Sometimes it feels like God needs a little help. Sometimes it seems like He has forgotten us. God will always keep his word, in his time. When we think we need to help God, we usually just make matters worse.

Father, give me the wisdom and discernment to know when you are calling me to action, and when I need to be waiting on you. Don't let me confuse the two.

By His grace,
Rick Weinert

Covenant, Flesh, Everlasting – Jan 14, 2011

In Genesis 17, God confirms his covenant with Abraham, establishing circumcision as the sign of the covenant. Regarding that sign he says, in verse 13b, "My covenant in your flesh is to be an everlasting covenant." There are three key words in this sentence: covenant, flesh, and everlasting. It's not often you see those three words together. "Covenant" and "everlasting" are words often connected, and sometimes "covenant" and "flesh" when circumcision is referenced. The words flesh and everlasting, however, are rarely heard in the same sentence, yet here we find it in Genesis 17. We may not be Gnostics, but we've largely bought into the Greek philosophy that spiritual is somehow better and higher than physical. For some Christians even the idea of Heaven being physical seems almost heretical. That's sad because, God created us to be both physical and spiritual beings. Every description of Heaven that we find in the Bible is a physical description so how have we developed this "spiritual" view of Heaven? Revelation 21 and 22 describe a New Heaven and New Earth. They describe nations bringing their "glory" to God in the City of Gold. We celebrate the Resurrection, but then spiritualize the resurrected body. Does the scripture say that our resurrected bodies will be changed? Yes. Does scripture say they will no longer be physical? No. God's covenant with Abraham was an eternal covenant in the flesh. Let's not over-spiritualize our faith. Let's be good Biblicists, not good Greek philosophers. To deny the value of the body is to deny the purpose and design of the creator. Genesis 17:13 is a good reminder of that.

Father, I don't want to idolize my body, nor try to preserve for ever that which is decaying because of sin. On the other hand, I don't want to deny an essential part of who you created me to be either. May I be a good steward of the body you have given me; may I celebrate and enjoy the body you have given me; may I keep my theology Biblical.

By His grace,
Rick Weinert

Genesis 18

Merciful Patience – Jan 15, 2011

There is so much of Abraham's culture in Genesis 18 that we may, or may not understand. What stands out to me though, in this chapter, is God's merciful patience. Why does he come to tell Abraham that the child will be born within a year? Why isn't he more upset with Sarah when she laughs at the idea of having a child at such an advanced age? Why is he willing to spare Sodom if only 10 righteous can be found in her? Merciful patience.

Father, thank you for your merciful patience in my life. May I be as merciful and patient with others.

By His grace,
Rick Weinert

Genesis 19

Influence & Obedience – Jan 17, 2011

As I read the story of the destruction of Sodom and Gomorrah, in Genesis 19, three things stand out to me. First, Lot was spared because of Abraham, even though he may never have known it. It makes me wonder how often, and to what extent, our families, our communities and our friends are impacted by our lives and our prayers even though they may not realize it. Second, Lot was told to go to the mountains but he asked permission to go to a nearby village instead. The permission was granted, but ultimately Lot ended up going to the mountains to live. How often do we ask God for a compromise, only to discover later that his original plan was where we would ultimately end up anyway? Wouldn't we be better off to simply say "yes" in the first place? The third thought that occurred to me was that if Lot's daughters had not seduced their father, then Israel would never have had to deal with the Moabites and the Ammonites. Sin often has much further reaching consequences than we ever realize. What makes sense to us in the fog of our sin crazed minds often leads to generations of pain.

I guess maybe the conclusion of all this is that I need to be quick to listen to God, quick to submit, and faithful to be an influence for His glory in my world. Father, I recognize that I can't do that on my own. By your grace, may that be true of me.

By His Grace,
Rick Weinert

Genesis 20

Covenant Grace – Jan 18, 2011

What a strange story of Abraham, Sarah, and Abimelech. Abraham tells the truth when he says that Sarah is his sister. She is his half sister. But, he tells the partial truth with the intent to deceive. He neglects the part about her being his wife. How does the story end? With Abraham getting wealthier, Sarah honored, and Abimelech's people restored. What's this about? We could draw all sorts of wrong conclusions from this if we're not careful, but one truth stands out. God is keeping his word. God had made a covenant with Abraham saying that he would bless him and multiply him. There were no conditions on Abraham in this covenant. What we see in this story is God blessing Abraham because of the covenant, in spite of Abraham's actions. This is a reminder that God will also keep the multiplying part of the covenant despite Abraham's earlier indiscretion with Hagar. Indeed, we will find Sarah giving birth to Isaac in the very next chapter.

Father, I am grateful for your grace and mercy by which you have often blessed me and my ministry in spite of me. Thank you! May I walk worthy of the grace you have so abundantly poured out on my life.

By His grace,
Rick Weinert

Genesis 21

Helping God – Jan 20, 2011

Genesis 21:10 NIV84

> (Sarah) said to Abraham, "Get rid of that slave woman and her son, for that slave woman's son will never share in the inheritance with my son Isaac."

"That slave woman's son" wouldn't even have been born had it not been for Sarah's decision to try and help God by giving her servant, Hagar, to Abraham. It seems that often the very thing we think we want becomes our undoing.

I recall a church that decided on what kind of man they wanted for their next pastor. They called a man that perfectly fit that profile, only to discover that wasn't what they wanted at all. The very thing that attracts a couple to one another can often become the thing that irritates them about one another. The toy, or tool, or gizmo that we think we need, to be effective, can sometimes distract us from effectiveness. The job, or position we think we need, to be successful, may be our undoing.

We need to be careful about the things we think we need, and the plans we make that seem so clear to us. How often have we tried to help God, only to discover that He didn't need our help at all, and we've made a mess of things? Father, may my heart be more tender to your Spirit, and less caught up in myself.

By His grace,
Rick Weinert

Genesis 22

God is Powerful and Good – Jan 21, 2011

In Genesis 22, God asked Abraham to sacrifice his son. Verse 10 says, "Abraham stretched out his hand and took the knife to slay his son." This raises all sorts of questions. How could God ask Abraham to do such a thing? Why would Abraham do such a thing? How could Abraham believe that God would really want him to do such a thing? Human sacrifice is a pagan practice. This is not the God of the Bible that we know. What's going on? What we forget is that, unlike a book or movie character, the characters of the Bible are not static, fully formed personalities. They are living, learning, growing people. Why would Abraham do such a thing, or believe that God would want him to do such a thing? We need to remember several things. First, Abraham lived in a culture that practiced human sacrifice. As abhorrent as the idea is, when a god speaks, you listen. Particularly when it is a god so powerful that he destroys cities and enables old women to have children. Second, we cannot assume that Abraham fully understood the nature and character of God. It was through this experience that Abraham came to understand God's principle of substitutionary death. But the biggest key to the story is in verse 5 when Abraham said to his servants, "Stay here with the donkey, and I and the lad will go over there; and we will worship and return to you." "We will ... return to you." Hebrews 11:19 comments, "He considered that God is able to raise people even from the dead..." Abraham didn't understand what was going on for sure. He was learning about this God he had been following for so many years, but he trusted him. He knew that God had said that he would multiply Abraham's seed through Isaac. If God wanted him to sacrifice Isaac then God must be planning to raise him from the dead. God could have done that, but he had an even better plan: a substitutionary sacrifice. Abraham learned that day that God is not only powerful, he is also good. Up until that day he had seen God's power. Now he has experienced his mercy and goodness as well. What a lesson Abraham learned, but think about the lesson Isaac learned. God loves you and has a wonderful plan for your life? Indeed!

Father, may I continue to learn and grow in my faith, as Abraham did. May I rest in your goodness and resurrection power, as did Abraham that day. May I walk in the wonder of your unrevealed plan for my life, as Isaac no doubt did beginning that day as he lay on the altar.

By His grace,
Rick Weinert

Genesis 23

Respect or Persecution – 22, 2011

In Genesis 23, we find the story of Sarah's death, and Abraham's purchase of property to bury her. I'm not sure there are any great spiritual lessons here, but it raises a couple interesting questions. Why is this story recorded for us? Why is Abraham buying land that God said he would give to Abraham? Why this long, polite interaction about the property? If Ephron wanted 400 shekels for his property, why didn't he just say so? What we get is an interesting glimpse into a culture that is very different from ours. This kind of interaction still goes on in some cultures today. It's all about respect.

The biggest question is, why did Abraham buy what God said he would give Abraham? Is Abraham back to his old habit of trying to help God? I don't think so. Rather, I think that Abraham is simply showing respect to the people he is living among. Liberty and independence is so ingrained in our American culture that the very idea of limiting our freedom for the sake of others is almost anathema. What we sometimes interpret as persecution is simply the consequences of our selfishness or stupidity. Abraham could have demanded that the cave be given to him because God said it was his. The result would not have been pretty. That is too often what we do, and call it persecution.

Father, give me the discernment to know how and when to limit my own freedom for the sake of your name and the good of others. Give me the grace to face persecution, but the wisdom not to confuse persecution with self inflicted conflict. Show me how to honour and respect others so that they might see Jesus in me.

By His grace,
Rick Weinert

Genesis 24

Isaac's Meditations – Jan 25, 2011

Genesis 24:63 NIV84

> "He went out to the field one evening to meditate, and as he looked up, he saw camels approaching."

Abraham's servant was sent to find a wife for Isaac. As he is bringing Rebecca home to be Isaac's wife, we find the verse quoted above. It makes you wonder what the focus of Isaac's thoughts were as he was waiting for a wife. I expect that he was wondering what this unknown woman would be like. But, as he is walking out in a field in the evening with the stars perhaps beginning to shine, do his thoughts go to the covenant God made with his father, Abraham? God said he would make Abraham's seed like the stars, but here is Isaac still waiting for a wife. Do his thoughts wander from there to the day Abraham tied him to an altar? Does he think back to the words of the angel that spared his life, and the ram caught in the bushes that became his substitute? Does he wonder about this God that led his father to this land? Abraham is getting very old. Is he overwhelmed with the prospect of taking responsibility for his father's wealth? Does he feel a bit melancholy as he thinks back to his mother, realizing that she is gone? Truthfully, we don't know the answers to any of these questions, but no doubt some of these things were on his mind. Was this evening meditation a regular habit of Isaac, or did he just happen to need a bit of time to think that evening? We don't know that either. What we do know is that as Isaac is meditating in the field Abraham's servant comes along with Rebecca. We know that Isaac took her to his mother's tent to be his wife, and we know that he loved her, and was comforted in his mother's death (see verse 67).

Two thoughts occured to me as I read this. The second thought that occurred to me was that God is good. He provided a wife for Isaac that comforted him and that he loved. He also provided the means by which he would fulfill his promise to Abraham. The first thought that occurred to me was simply the thought that I probably spend too much time with my phone, the internet, and the television, and too little time just thinking and listening in the presence of God. I doubt that's the application God had in mind when he inspired this verse to be written, but then you never know. What I do know is that Jesus made it a habit to go out to the wilderness alone with the Father, and I do know that I need to do more of that myself.

By His grace,
Rick Weinert

Genesis 25

Today's Choices – Tomorrow's Consequences – Jan 26, 2011

Genesis 25 is the set up for the rest of the story. Many of the conflicts that will come find their roots in this chapter. Abraham has other children from another wife. Among them we find Midian. Ishmael's family grows, as God promised. Joseph will be sold to Midianites and Ismaelites in Genesis 37. Gideon, in the book of Judges, will find himself up against the Midianites. Abraham is already becoming the Father of many nations, but he is also setting up the story for much conflict. Isaac has twins, Esau and Jacob. Further conflict is on the horizon between these two, particularly as we see Jacob favored by his mother and Esau favored by his father. Further, we see Esau's impulsive lifestyle.

Can God change lives? Absolutely! We will watch God mold and transform Isaac, Jacob, Joseph and others as the story progresses. But, we also see that our actions have consequences. Decisions today affect actions, issues, and even conflicts of tomorrow. We can't see the future, but we can live with the future in mind, knowing that each decision I make today will impact the decisions I face tomorrow. Father, don't let me become paralyzed by that thought. Rather, give me the wisdom and discernment to make wise choices, and to live with eternity in mind.

By His grace,
Rick Weinert

Genesis 26

Evidence of God's Presence – Jan 27, 2011

Genesis 26:28 NIV84

"We saw clearly that the Lord was with you; so we said, 'There ought to be a sworn agreement between us' — between us and you. Let us make a treaty with you"

Earlier in the chapter Isaac had been fearful of the Philistines, but now, according to the next couple verses, they have become fearful of him. They have recognized that God is with him and blessing him. That made me begin to wonder what there is in my life that might indicate to those around me that God is with me.

The Spirit filled life produces the fruit of the Spirit. The God focused life is characterized by peace. It's not wealth and power, but love, joy, peace, patience, kindness, goodness, faithfulness, gentleness, self control ... These are the sorts of things that indicate the presence of God in a life. If these things aren't growing in my life then I need to re-examine my own fellowship with God or I'll be hard pressed to convince anyone else that God is with me.

Father, may my life reflect Jesus to those around me, to your glory.

By His grace,
Rick Weinert

Genesis 27

Knowing God – Jan 28, 2011

Jacob was a schemer, but he seems to have come by it naturally. His mother, Rebecca, was a bit of a schemer herself. In Genesis 27, we find the story of Jacob stealing Esau's blessing. Rebecca is the one that plans and initiates the scheme. What strikes me, as I read the story, is that no one seems to be concerned about the ethics of the scheme. Jacob is only concerned about getting caught. Why is that?

Genesis 27:11-12 NIV84

> Jacob said to Rebekah his mother, "But my brother Esau is a hairy man, and I'm a man with smooth skin. What if my father touches me? I would appear to be tricking him and would bring down a curse on myself rather than a blessing."

Perhaps the answer is found in verse 20, where Jacob refers to Isaac's God. He doesn't say, "our God." He says, "your God." Jacob has not yet come to know God. He only knows about him. It will take several more years, a vision of a stairway to heaven, and a night wrestling with God before God will be Jacob's God.

Father, thank you that, by your grace, my Dad's God is mine. Thank you that you are also the God of my children. May you be the God of my grandchildren and great grandchildren as well. May our generations, until you return, know you as their God.

By His grace,
Rick Weinert

Genesis 29

Security, Significance & Satisfaction – Jan 31, 2011

Genesis 29:30-31 NIV84

> "Jacob lay with Rachel also, and he loved Rachel more than Leah. And he worked for Laban another seven years. When the Lord saw that Leah was not loved, he opened her womb, but Rachel was barren."

These verses are followed by the record of Leah having four sons. After the birth of each of the first three she expresses the hope that perhaps now she will be loved by her husband. Finally, after the birth of the fourth son she seems to have given up that hope and turns her thoughts to God.

Genesis 29:35a NIV84

> "She conceived again, and when she gave birth to a son she said, "This time I will praise the Lord.""

Why is it so difficult for us to come to that place where we say, "This time I will praise the Lord"? We are constantly looking to people, circumstances and stuff for the affirmation and meaning that we must ultimately find in Christ.

Leah has learned a good lesson here. Jacob has a lesson to learn as well. While Rachel may be the more beautiful of the two, it will be Rachel who clings to her father's idols, stealing them when they leave Laban. Leah sought the significance of being loved, and apparently came to find that in the Lord. Jacob sought the satisfaction of a beautiful wife. Rachel sought the security of her father's idols. To begin with they were all looking in the wrong place to fill these basic yearnings.

Father, I confess that my default is to look to people, circumstances, roles and opportunities, and stuff, when I should be looking to you. My security, significance and satisfaction can only be found, in any lasting and meaningful way, in you Lord.

By His grace,
Rick Weinert

Genesis 30

Blessed Because of Jesus – Feb 1, 2011

Genesis 30:43 NIV84

> "In this way the man grew exceedingly prosperous and came to own large flocks, and maidservants and menservants, and camels and donkeys."

In Genesis 30, we find God increasing Jacob's family and wealth. There is nothing particularly godly about Jacob at this point in his life. His wives are fighting over him. He is using tricks to try and increase his flocks. While Laban recognizes that, "the Lord has blessed me because of you," Jacob seems to totally miss that point. So why does God bless him? Because of the covenant that he made with Abraham and Isaac.

The same is true of us. If God is blessing us, we tend to attribute it to our faith, or obedience, or personal holiness. If we don't feel blessed we wonder what we've done wrong. The truth is, any blessing we experience is because of Christ, not because of us. Every joy we experience, every moment of peace, every blessing of provision is an aspect of God's mercy and grace.

Father, I rest in your grace and thank you for every blessing. Forgive me for the times when I somehow begin to think that this is about me. It's all about Jesus. Thank you!

By His grace,
Rick Weinert

Genesis 31

The Fear of Isaac – Feb 2, 2011

Twice in Genesis 31 Jacob refers to God as "the fear of his father Isaac." I have preached, and heard, many sermons on names of God. I don't think I've ever heard a sermon based on the name, "The Fear of Isaac."

We like to think of God as loving, and he is. But we forget that the Jesus John was so familiar with at the last supper is the same Jesus at whose feet he "fell as though dead"in Revelation 1. We forget that Jesus, who loved us enough to die for us, is the same Jesus that will "judge the living and the dead." We forget that God, who spared Lot and his family from the destruction of Sodom, is the same God that sent the destruction against Sodom. God is both approachable and unapproachable; he is both fearsome and gentle; he is a God of love and justice, judgment and mercy.

God is no Santa Claus. Neither is he an uncaring tyrant. When we begin to think of him as one or the other, losing the biblical balance, we have created a new god and impose expectations on God that are not accurate.

Father, forgive me for the times I have gotten out of balance, the times I have laughingly run into your presence when I should have bowed at your feet, and the times I have cowered in fear when I should have been resting in your gentle love. Thank you for this reminder that "The Fear of Isaac" blessed and protected Jacob.

By His grace,
Rick Weinert

Genesis 32

Desperation – Feb 4, 2011

In Genesis 32, Jacob sent a message to his brother Esau, to let him know that he was coming home. When he heard that Esau was headed his way with 400 men, he was fearful and prayed this prayer:

Genesis 32:10-11 NIV84

> "I am unworthy of all the kindness and faithfulness you have shown your servant. I had only my staff when I crossed this Jordan, but now I have become two groups. Save me, I pray, from the hand of my brother Esau, for I am afraid he will come and attack me, and also the mothers with their children."

Perhaps for the first time in his life he has expressed the truth of his own unworthiness and desperate need. This is the point where God meets us. When we still think it's about what we deserve, or what we can scheme our way out of, we haven't come to the point of needing God on his terms. Jacob has finally learned that his wealth was a gift from God, not a result of his own con. He is desperate, not only to save his own skin, but to save the lives of "the mothers and their children." Somehow these are hard lessons for us to learn. God must bring us to the end of ourselves.

Father, you have always been there in the darkest times of my life. You have met me often in my desperation. May my heart not grow cold in the comfortable times.

By His grace,
Rick Weinert

Genesis 33

Transformation – Feb 5, 2011

Genesis 33:19 NIV84

> "For a hundred pieces of silver, he bought from the sons of Hamor, the father of Shechem, the plot of ground where he pitched his tent."

This passage is the first place in scripture where I recall anyone buying property on which to pitch their tent. In this chapter, Jacob gives flocks and herds to his brother in reconciliation, and purchases property for his tents. No more scheming. No more cons. Jacob is a new man.

We often excuse bad behavior with the phrase, "I can't help it. That's just who I am." This is no excuse. God is in the business of transforming lives. Father, forgive me for the times I have attempted to excuse sin and bad behavior with just such an excuse. May I reflect your glory and your truth today. Continue to faithfully transform my life into the image of Christ.

Genesis 34

Contentment or Greed – Feb 7, 2011

I read Genesis 34 today. I read it yesterday too. Some passages take me a couple days of thinking on them before I seem to be able to make any sense out of them. I'm still wrestling a bit with this chapter trying to figure out why it is here. Maybe in the bigger picture of the whole story it makes sense in some way. If I recall, it plays back into the story in some way later, but I'm not sure there are any great spiritual lessons here. We have a tendency to read passages like this through the lens of our own culture. Understanding what is really going on in their culture is much more difficult, but clearly, as verse 7 points out, "Shechem had done a disgraceful thing in Israel." That being said, after reading it two days, it did occur to me that the lust and selfishness of Shechem and their people led to their downfall.

The story starts with Shechem raping, and then asking to marry Dinah because "His heart was drawn to" her. (Gen 34:3) When Dinah's brothers hear what has happened, they hatch a plan. They ask Shechem and all their men to be circumcised. If they agree to this then, they will let Shechem marry Dinah and they will intermarry with the whole group. Shechem's words to his friends are revealing. In verse 23 he argues the benefits of going along with this plan. "Won't their livestock, their property and all their other animals become ours? So let us give our consent to them, and they will settle among us." All the men agree. Three days later they were all killed and their wealth and families were carried off by Dinah's brothers. Greed caused their downfall.

Father, forgive me for the times I have allowed my yearnings and greed for more stuff to color my decisions and choices. May I, with the Apostle Paul, be content in whatever circumstances I find myself.

By His grace,
Rick Weinert

Genesis 35

Generational Faith – Feb 8, 2011

Genesis 35 is the first place where Jacob does not refer to God as "the God of my fathers." He is just "God." Here God passes on to Jacob the Abrahamic Covenant and a new name, Israel. Each generation must encounter and know God for themselves. Abraham met God and was promised blessing. Isaac met God and the promise to Abraham was passed to him. Now Jacob has come to know God and become a recipient of the promise. It is clear, however, that his family does not yet know God. They bury their idols not out of conviction, but by Jacob's command. Their hearts have clearly not been touched, as evidenced by Reuben's immoral act with Bilah, his father's concubine. This is a good reminder that my faith is not automatically transferred to my children and grandchildren.

By God's grace, my children are all walking with the Lord. I pray daily for their protection, and that this would be true of my grandchildren and great-grandchildren as well. Father, let it be so. Amen!

By His grace,
Rick Weinert

Genesis 36

Rest & Responsibility – Feb 9, 2011

Genesis 36 is a record of Esau's descendants and the rulers of Edom. Reading through the chapter, two thoughts occur to me. First is that God is fulfilling his promise to Abraham to make him the father of many nations. Second is the fact that several of Esau's descendants become the nations that oppose the Sons of Israel when they exit from Egypt. Perhaps a lesson from this chapter is simply that God blesses us because of his word, not because of who we are.

I am grateful for that truth. When we do great things, we can be reminded that it is by His grace, not our greatness. I believe it was Howard Hendricks who said to our class in seminary, "Never believe your press reports." That's good advice.

On the other hand, when we blow it, we can rest in the truth that God will accomplish his purpose in spite of us. This is no excuse for mediocrity, nor irresponsibility, but it is reassuring. Were eternity to rest solely on my shoulders, the world would be in a "world of hurt."

Father, help me to keep that proper balance between rest and responsibility, between dependent humility and faithful ministry.

By His grace,
Rick Weinert

Genesis 37

Can't Stop God – Feb 10, 2011

Genesis 37:20 NIV84I

> "Come now, let's kill him and throw him into one of these cisterns and say that a ferocious animal devoured him. Then we'll see what comes of his dreams."

Joseph's brothers are jealous of him and plot his demise. They end up selling him to traders on their way to Egypt. Little do they understand, of course, that they are playing right into God's plan. It will be because Joseph is in Epypt that their families will survive a famine in coming years.

Two lessons stand out to me in this chapter. First is that God used them to accomplish his purposes despite their character and motives. Second is that evil men could not stop God's will. Yesterday, I received an urgent prayer request from missionary friends. They had a huge outreach planned and suddenly the building they planned to use was no longer available. Today, I received an email indicating God's better provision, a building available at no cost. Praise the Lord! Sometimes the very thing we fear most becomes the vehicle for God's blessing and provision.

Father, forgive me for how often the problems and obstacles of this world are more real to me than you are. May I rest in your sovereign care.

By His grace,
Rick Weinert

Genesis 38

Hypocrisy & Humility – Feb 14, 2011

The hypocrisy of Judah, in Genesis 38, is glaring. Not realizing that the prostitute at the side of the road is really his daughter-in-law, Judah sleeps with Tamar. When he later discovers that she is pregnant, and is guilty of prostitution, he is ready to have her burned to death. Yet at the root of the whole mess was his own sin, and he had committed the very sin for which she was being judged. Hypocrisy is the very thing that Jesus would condemn the Scribes and Pharisees for generations later.

As believers, we are quite ready to condemn and castigate the Pharisees. It makes me wonder, though, how pharisaical we are. Do we condemn Tamar, all the while being Judah? Father, I fear that I might actually be the Pharisee I so passionately rebuke. Don't let me get away with that. Thank you for Judah's response when he finally figures out the child is his, "She is more righteous than I." Father, may my eyes be open to recognize this, and may I be as quick to admit my own sin.

By His grace,
Rick Weinert

Genesis 39

Pure Eyes – Feb 15, 2011

Genesis 39:12 NIV84

> "She caught him by his cloak and said, "Come to bed with me!" But he left his cloak in her hand and ran out of the house."

Few men, to my knowledge, have women throwing themselves at them. That is, not as directly as this. But in our society, women are increasingly throwing themselves at men indirectly through television, advertising, the internet, movies, pornography, etc. Rather than fleeing, or even just diverting our eyes, we too often just keep staring at the screen. If you are a man, when was the last time you looked only at the face of a woman? Women are not exempt from this either. Women are a fast growing segment of the pornography market.

Job said he had made a covenant with his eyes not to look lustfully at a woman. It's too bad David hadn't done that before Bathsheba. Father, may I keep my eyes and my mind pure. By your grace may I look away and set my mind on you. May I be a Job and a Joseph, not a David, in these matters.

By His grace,
Rick Weinert

Genesis 40

Hope in Darkness – Feb 16, 2011

Genesis 40:23 NIV84

> "The chief cupbearer, however, did not remember Joseph; he forgot him."

Joseph helped this guy out in prison. He asked to be remembered, but he was forgotten. You know the old saying, no good deed goes unpunished. The truth is, not every good deed is immediately rewarded. Sometimes, when we do the right thing, things get darker. But God...

God was just as sovereign when Joseph was falsely accused, and later forgotten, as he was when Joseph was elevated to being in charge of Potiphar's household, or when he was finally released from prison and made Pharoah's number one man. God was just as much in control when my friend's vehicle went over the side of the mountain as when my car straightened out after sliding sideways down the highway, or when one man gets a new job and another loses his home.

I don't understand these things, but I know that God never stops being God. In the darkest times, we sometimes feel the most alone, and other times we most feel the presence of God, but either way He is there in the darkness. I wonder how Joseph felt waiting there in prison hoping to be remembered. I wonder if there were times when he gave up hope.

Father, thank you that you are there in the darkest times just as you are in times of hope, peace and freedom. When life gets dark may I turn to your light.

By His grace,
Rick Weinert

Genesis 41

God's Timing – Feb 17, 2011

Genesis 41:1, 9, 44 NIV84

> "When two full years had passed, Pharaoh had a dream: He was standing by the Nile, ... Then the chief cupbearer said to Pharaoh, "Today I am reminded of my shortcomings. ... Then Pharaoh said to Joseph, "I am Pharaoh, but without your word no one will lift hand or foot in all Egypt.""

God's timing is not our timing. In the previous chapter Joseph had interpreted a dream for the cupbearer, and asked to be remembered when he was released. The cupbearer forgot about him for two years until this dream of Pharoah's. Joseph would have preferred a quick release from prison, but God's timing is not ours. No doubt Joseph could not even imagine the life he was about to fall into. He just wanted out of prison, but God had other plans.

Clearly not all of us are going to go from dark times to ruling a country, but if we are willing to walk the path God calls us to, we may be surprised by where it takes us and whom we influence for the Kingdom. But, we must be patient. Everything in God's time, not ours. God is never in a hurry.

When we are in positions of leadership, God often gives us a vision of where we need to go as an organization or movement before we are actually ready to go there. If we get impatient or try to push our agenda, before those we are leading have been prepared for it, we can do more damage than good. If we are walking through dark times and try to find shortcuts to a solution, we often dig ourselves a deeper hole. Lessons are learned slowly. We need to give God time to work.

Father, Moses spent forty years in the backside of the wilderness after he first caught the vision for freeing his people. Joseph sat in prison for two years before you made it clear why he was there. Forgive me for my own impatience. Father, in your time may you glorify your name through me however you choose. In the mean time, may I be patiently faithful in that which you have put before me to do.

By His grace,
Rick Weinert

Genesis 42

Hope in the Darkness – Feb 18, 2011

In Genesis 42, Jacob sends his sons to Egypt to buy food. The trip results in Simeon being held in prison and the demand for Benjamin to be brought there as well. Jacob responds, "Everything is against me." Of course what he does not realize is that salvation is at his doorstep. He can't see past the pain and the fear. I wonder how often God has great blessing waiting in the darkness, but we give up because of pain and fear.

Father, I don't like those dark times you take us through, but I trust you. May I find in you the grace to walk whatever path you put before me, and may I meet you in the darkness.

By His grace,
Rick Weinert

Genesis 43

Taking Responsibility – Feb 19, 2011

Genesis 43:8-9 NIV84

> "Then Judah said to Israel his father, "... you can hold me personally responsible for him. If I do not bring

him back to you and set him here before you, I will bear the blame before you all my life."

Back in chapter 37, it was Judah's idea to sell Joseph into slavery. In chapter 42 it is Reuben, not Judah who offers to take responsibility for Benjamin's life. Finally, in this chapter we find Judah taking some responsibility.

Sin is bad. Cover-up is worse. We bring so much pain into our lives and the lives of those we love when we are not willing to come clean about our sin. How many years have they been carrying the guilt of their actions against Joseph? How has that affected their relationships with their father, their families, and with each other?

Father, may I walk in holiness and purity, but when I do sin may I come clean quickly, for your sake and that of those I love.

By His grace,
Rick Weinert

Genesis 44

Forgiveness or Guilt – Feb 21, 2011

Genesis 44:16 NIV84

> "What can we say to my lord?" Judah replied. "What can we say? How can we prove our innocence? God has uncovered your servants' guilt. We are now my lord's slaves—we ourselves and the one who was found to have the cup."

They were innocent of any theft from the Egyptians, but they had been carrying the guilt of what they had done to Joseph for years. "God has uncovered your servants' guilt." Guilt is a heavy burden to carry. That's what makes the gospel such good news. Forgiveness is not about ignoring and overlooking sin. Forgiveness is about washing us clean. If God's forgiveness was simply about winking at our indiscretions, then the death of Jesus was unnecessary and cruel. God's forgiveness, however, is rooted deeply in his own personal holiness. Through the death of Jesus, God's holiness is satisfied, his justice untarnished, and his love for us demonstrated. Judah hasn't quite figured that out yet, but he has taken the first step.

Father, thank you for your forgiveness. May I walk in the rest of your forgiveness rather than in the burden of my guilt. May I have opportunities to share that rest with others.

By His grace,
Rick Weinert

Genesis 45

God's Love – Feb 22, 2011

Genesis 45:5 NIV84

> "And now, do not be distressed and do not be angry with yourselves for selling me here, because it was to save lives that God sent me ahead of you."

Three thoughts come to mind as I think on this verse. First, God uses even sinners and sinful decisions to accomplish his purposes. The brothers acted out of jealousy when they sold Joseph into slavery, but God used it for his purposes.

Second, God used that event to save sinners. The end result was not just the physical salvation of Jacob, but of the very men who sold Joseph in the first place. God's ways are not our ways, and God's favor is never merited on our part. We do not deserve his mercy and grace.

Finally, this is what Jesus did for us. He was sent ahead of us to save our lives. We now have the privilege and responsibility to take that good news to others.

Father, I realize that I have often taken your mercy and grace for granted. Forgive me. May I walk today in a fuller appreciation of your love for me and for those around me.

By His grace,
Rick Weinert

Genesis 46

Listening Well – Feb 23, 2011

Genesis 46:3 NIV84

> ""I am God, the God of your father," he said. "Do not be afraid to go down to Egypt, for I will make you into a great nation there."

Jacob's grandfather, Abraham, was not to go to Egypt. Jacob's descendents will be told not to go to Egypt. Here God assures Jacob that going to Egypt is the right thing to do. There are some things that are always right, and some things that are always wrong. There are other things that are right for one person and wrong for another. The New Testament tells us, "Anyone, then, who knows the good he ought to do and doesn't do it, sins." (James 4:17)

Father, I want to stay close enough to you that I am able to hear clearly what you are calling me to do. Forgive me for those times when I have known I should do something, and have neglected to follow through. May I never act only out of consensus, or because that's what we've always done. May I listen carefully, and follow you faithfully.

By His grace,
Rick Weinert

Genesis 47

Giving – Feb 24, 2011

Genesis 47:26 NIV84

> "So Joseph established it as a law concerning land in Egypt—still in force today—that a fifth of the

produce belongs to Pharaoh. It was only the land of the priests that did not become Pharaoh's."

The flocks and herds all belong to Pharaoh. The land belongs to Pharaoh, and he demands a fifth of the crops. This reminds me that all I have belongs to God. None of my stuff is mine. My most precious possessions are not mine, they are His. My life, my health, my home, all that I am and all that I have are God's. But God is not nearly such a hard taskmaster. The tithe was a reminder of this truth. God asked for only half as much as Joseph demanded on behalf of Pharaoh.

Regular, planned giving to God is not so much about supporting the ministry. God doesn't really need our money to accomplish his purposes. Nor is it just a religious duty. It is an act of worship. Not because it makes us feel a particular way. Giving is an act of worship because it acknowledges God as Lord, master of all I am and have. When I write that check, or send that money, or drop cash in the plate, I am recognizing that none of this stuff is mine. God has blessed me with the use of it, and I am called to be a good steward of what is his. I am not giving God some of my money. I am keeping most of his money. Giving reminds me of that.

Father, I realize that all I have is yours. Forgive me for not being as faithful in my giving as I ought to be. May I faithfully bow the knee before you and acknowledge you through my giving.

By His grace,
Rick Weinert

Genesis 48

Generational Faith – Feb 25, 2011

Genesis 48:3, 9 NIV84

"Jacob said to Joseph, "God Almighty appeared to me at Luz in the land of Canaan, and there he blessed me

"They are the sons God has given me here," Joseph said to his father.Then Israel said, "Bring them to me so I may bless them.""

In this chapter, Jacob is passing on a heritage of faith to his grandchildren. As a child, my grandparents had a huge impact on my life. It is a blessed and awe filled role grandparents play in passing on, or in some cases beginning, a heritage of faith.

The disintegration of the family has made this more difficult. Older believers may find that we need to fill that need in the lives of children who do not have anyone like that in their lives. As a grandfather, I need to be intentional about spending time with my grandchildren and modelling Jesus for them. I don't want to be preaching at them, but I certainly need to be praying and watching for opportunities to pass on my faith to them.

Father, I am honoured and privileged that you would entrust me with children and grandchildren. May I be a model of holiness and an influence for faith in their lives.

By His grace,
Rick Weinert

Genesis 28

Thoughts on Genesis 28 – Feb 26, 2011

As I read Genesis 28, four thoughts occur to me. First, how did I miss this chapter? I realized yesterday that somehow, in my blogging through Genesis, I skipped this chapter, so I decided to go back and read it today. What a rich passage.

Second, Genesis 28:8 says,

"Esau then realized how displeasing the Canaanite women were to his father Isaac."

It appears that even though Esau realized that the Canaanite women were displeasing to his father, he didn't really understand why. It reminds me of a couple I counselled for marriage several years ago. After two hours of talking about the significance of marriage and the role of sex in marriage the young woman blurted out, "So that's why my parents are so upset about us living together. I knew they were upset, but I didn't understand why." If we pass on rules to the next generation without the reasons, we set up our children for rebellion, or at least some very bad decisions.

My third thought is based on Genesis 28:14b

"All peoples on earth will be blessed through you and your offspring."

This was the promise God made to Abraham. He passed the promise on to Isaac, and now to Jacob. It is through the death and resurrection of Jesus, a descendent of Abraham, Isaac and Jacob, that this promise is fulfilled. As believers in Jesus Christ, we then have the privilege and responsibility of taking that blessing to the world. I wonder how many people view the presence of Christians as a blessing.

The last thought that occurred to me came from Genesis 28:22a

"This stone that I have set up as a pillar will be God's house"

I understand the need to have someplace to go to when we worship God. That seems to be a relatively universal concept. Unfortunately by doing that, we often relegate God to one place and one time in our experience. Jacob needed to learn that when he left Bethel, he didn't leave God. All of life should be worship. That seems to be a hard lesson to learn.

By His grace,

Genesis 49

Our Strength – Feb 28, 2011

In the midst of Jacob blessing his sons, just before his death, we find this verse:

Genesis 49:24 NIV84

> "But his bow remained steady, his strong arms stayed limber, because of the hand of the Mighty One of Jacob, because of the Shepherd, the Rock of Israel."

Jacob is referring to Joseph in this passage. Joseph's strength is not found in his strong personality, or his personal strength, but in the strength of the God who holds him.

Strength, patience, holiness, effectiveness, power are not found in us, but in the hands of the God who holds us. As the song goes, "You are my strength when I am weak ... You are my all in all." But it is not only in our weakness that God is our strength. Even in our strength, God is our strength. When we forget this and begin to feel competent in ourselves, apart from God, we set ourselves up for failure and disappointment.

Father, thank you that you are my strength, not only when I am weak, but when I am strong as well. In you I rest.

By His grace,
Rick Weinert

Remembrance & Faith

Genesis 50:25 NIV84

"And Joseph made the sons of Israel swear an oath and said, "God will surely come to your aid, and then you must carry my bones up from this place.""

This was an act of faith on Joseph's part. He could just as easily have asked to be taken back immediately for burial like they did for Jacob. Joseph has seen God sovereignly accomplish his purposes throughout his lifetime. He assures his brothers, "You intended to harm me, but God intended it for good." Surely this statement to his brothers has brought back memories of his journey from favored son to slave, to prisoner, to Pharoah's right hand man, to a restored family. Joseph is confident that God will keep his promise made to Abraham back in Genesis 15.

Father thank you for the reminders you give us of your faithfulness. The Lord's Supper is a reminder of your love and faithfulness. Forgive us for turning it into a religious rite. May we, with Joseph, look back, remember, and then step out in faith.

By His grace,
Rick Weinert